DO Not Eat This Book!

FUN WITH JEWISH FOODS & FESTIVALS

WRITTEN BY
Beth Kander

ILLUSTRATED BY
Mike Moran

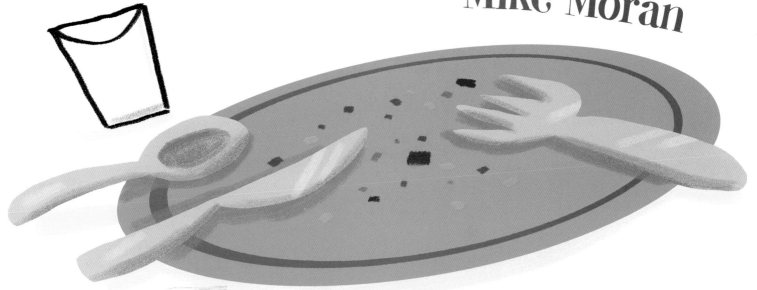

PUBLISHED BY SLEEPING BEAR PRESS™

Almost every Jewish holiday
comes with a special food
full of smells and flavors
that set a festive mood.

Let's see what's on the table;
come take a closer look—

but please remember, bubbeleh:

DO NOT EAT THIS BOOK!

Tu B'Shevat is so much fun,
a new year for the trees!
Figs and nuts and dates, oh yum!
A second helping, please.

On **Purim** we read a story,
we call out boos and cheers,
and eat a special cookie
named after someone's ears....

I know you're getting hungry,
seeing yummy things we cook—
but please remember, bubbeleh:
DO NOT EAT THIS BOOK!

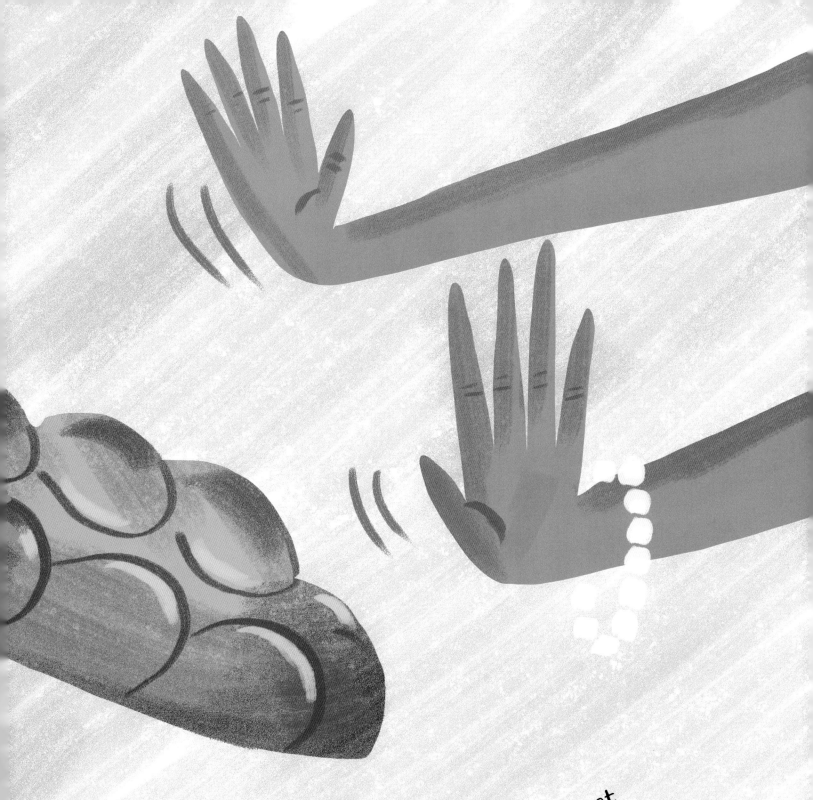

Each **Shabbat** brings lovely rest
and a special braided bread
so good you might skip dinner
and just eat challah instead!

Every culture in the world
has special festive foods,
reflecting hopes and histories
in every bite that's chewed.

Can you think of a special dish
your family loves to cook?
Maybe you will eat that soon

(but DO NOT EAT THIS BOOK!).

The special thing about our foods
in all their tasty glories
is the way they can connect us
and tell such delicious stories.

When we're together, we give thanks
for the things that make life sweet.
We talk, we laugh, we sing, we dance
(and yes, of course, we always eat).

SO REMEMBER . . .

You may hear your tummy rumble!

Oh, how mouthwatering the pages look!

But please remember, bubbeleh:

DO NOT EAT
THIS BOOK!

Glossary

Bubbeleh (Yiddish): *Bubbeleh* is a sweet nickname like *darling* or *sweetie*. Anyone who calls you that thinks you're delightful, and possibly delicious.

Chanukah (Hebrew): *Chanukah*—also spelled Hanukkah, and many other ways!—means "dedication." It is a winter holiday, also called "the festival of lights," for the beautiful candles we kindle commemorating the rededication of the Temple when the Maccabees won it back, and the miracle of the oil that lasted for eight nights instead of just one.

Purim (Hebrew): *Purim* means "lots," for the lots drawn by the evil Haman to determine the fate of the Jewish people. Queen Esther and her cousin Mordechai saved the Jewish people from Haman's wicked plots, and now we celebrate with costumes, carnivals, and fun foods!

Seder (Hebrew): *Seder* means "order." It's what we call the Passover celebration, since there is a set order to how we celebrate at the seder table.

Shabbat (Hebrew): *Shabbat* means "sabbath." It's the seventh day of the week. We learn that God rested on the seventh day after creating the world, so on the seventh day of each week, we take a break to rest, too!

Shavuot (Hebrew): Traditionally a harvest holiday, Shavuot is now when we celebrate the Jewish people receiving the Torah. We eat a lot of delicious dairy (or dairy-like) foods.

Tu B'Shevat (Hebrew): *Tu B'Shevat* means the "Fifteenth of Shevat"—it's a holiday whose name is also its date, like the Fourth of July. Just like the Fourth of July is also called Independence Day, Tu B'Shevat is also called *Rosh Hashanah La'Ilanot*, "New Year of the Trees." It is now also celebrated as an ecological holiday when we plant trees and do things to help take care of the planet.

Author's Note

Every culture has wonderful foods to share! The foods associated with Jewish holidays often connect directly with the stories, traditions, and meanings of the celebrations. There are so many delicious, diverse dishes in the Jewish world. Whether a Jewish family is Ashkenazic, Sephardic, or Karaite; chose Judaism; or has a Jewish identity intertwined with other cultures, the foods we eat tell us so many stories about our past, present, and future. By exploring culinary traditions, we learn so much about history, heritage, and more. On the following pages you'll find some fun, kid-friendly Jewish recipes to share with your family throughout the year ahead. (And yes, bubbeleh, this is the part where you get to eat!)

Tu B'Shevat

Build a CHARCUTER-TREE!

Tu B'Shevat is the New Year for trees! This holiday reminds us just how important nature is; we are all responsible for taking care of our planet. You may have heard the word *charcuterie*, which can mean a tray with lots of different foods. One fun way your family can experience Tu B'Shevat through food is to create a "Charcuter-Tree," incorporating some of the traditional foods like grapes, figs, and pomegranates! Here's an easy way to build your own Tu B'Shevat Charcuter-Tree.

How to Make Your
CHARCUTER-TREE

1. Get a lot of fruits and veggies.

2. Chop up into small pieces to build your tree.

3. ENJOY!

Purim

THE EASIEST HAMENTASCHEN!

On Purim, it's easy to get caught up in all the celebrations. Costumes! Carnivals! Purim spiels! But of course, we can't forget the foods. Hamentaschen are probably the most famous Purim food. If you don't have time to make dough from scratch, this easy recipe lets you quickly enjoy freshly baked hamentaschen!

How to Make the
EASIEST HAMENTASCHEN

2 eggs

1 cup fruit preserves

2 tablespoons water

FLOUR

1 cup flour

1 box (15.25 ounces) moist yellow cake mix

DIRECTIONS: Preheat oven to 375°F and put parchment paper on two cookie sheets. In a large bowl, combine cake mix and flour. Stir in eggs and water. On a lightly floured surface, roll the dough out 1/8-inch thick. Cut into 3-inch round circles. Place 1 teaspoon of fruit filling in the center of each cookie; pinch sides to form three corners. Bake for 6 to 8 minutes, then allow 1 minute of cooling time before transferring to wire racks for more cooling.

Shabbat

SHAKSHUKA

Bubbelehs, have you ever tried shakshuka? It's a popular Israeli dish—and a great introduction to Middle Eastern food because it features eggs, tomatoes, and can be altered to your household's desired spice level (including a spice level of zero).

How to Make
ŚHABBAT ŚHAKSHUKA

1 24-ounce jar
of tomato sauce

pinches of your favorite
spices: garlic, salt, pepper,
coriander, etc.

6 to 8 eggs

optional: feta cheese

optional: cilantro, parsley,
torn basil for garnish

DIRECTIONS: Pour the jar of tomato sauce into a skillet or large, deep frying pan. Bring to a gentle simmer. With a spoon, create little "nests" for each egg, then crack them and place one in each nest (this is best done by a grown-up). If you like feta cheese, crumble some over the eggs. Then cover the dish and allow the eggs to steam-cook to your preferred texture—soft, hard, or in-between. You can also add spices and garnish—or not, if your young chefs prefer their shakshuka sans spice!

PaSSover

MATZAH MAC & CHEESE

For Passover, we avoid eating *chametz* (leavened foods) to remind us of how quickly the Jewish people fled Egypt to seek freedom. Using matzah-based ingredients all week is a fun challenge; dishes like this Matzah Mac & Cheese make that challenge truly tasty!

How to Make
MATZAH MAĆ

DIRECTIONS: Preheat the oven to 350°F. Grease a 9-inch x 13-inch baking dish (or any dish big enough for whole squares of matzah). In a bowl, whisk together the eggs, milk, salt, and pepper. Dip squares of matzah into the milk mixture, then place 2 on the bottom of the baking dish. Start layering: dipped matzah, sour cream, cheddar cheese. Repeat the process three times, layering dipped matzah squares, sour cream, and cheese. Add one last layer of matzah for a total of 4 layers. Top with the remaining sour cream, pour any remaining milk mixture over it all, then add all the mozzarella cheese. Bake, covered with foil, for 35 minutes, then uncovered for 5 minutes. Let rest for 5 minutes and serve!

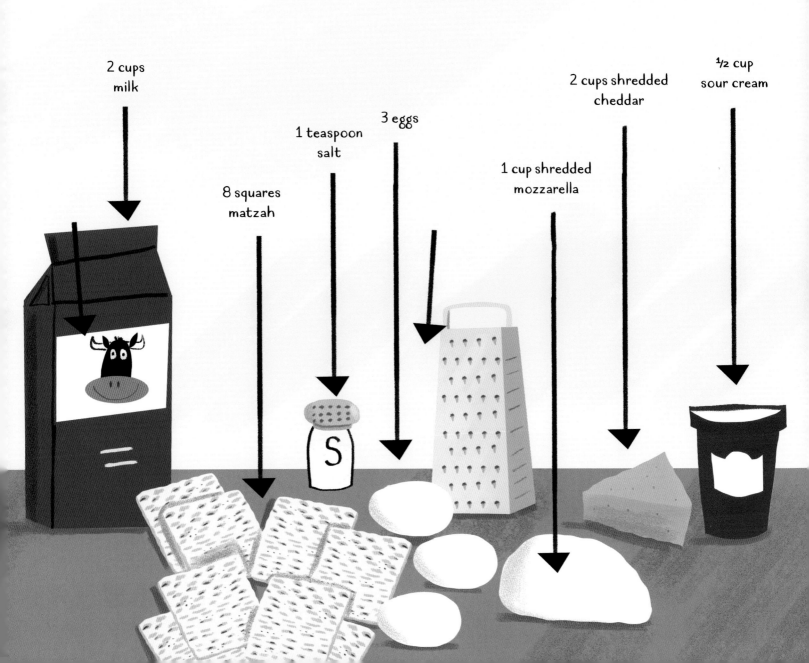

2 cups
milk

8 squares
matzah

1 teaspoon
salt

3 eggs

1 cup shredded
mozzarella

2 cups shredded
cheddar

½ cup
sour cream

Shavuot

ICE CREAM IN A BAG

Since Shavuot was a harvest holiday, it has always had a direct connection to food. One tradition now is to eat a lot of delicious dairy foods. Blintzes are one yummy tradition—but for an easy, fun, delicious Shavuot treat, you've got to try Ice Cream in a Bag!

How to Make
ICE CREAM IN A BAG

1 cup half-and-half

¼ cup salt

2 resealable plastic bags

1 tablespoon sugar

ice cubes

1½ tablespoon vanilla

DIRECTIONS: Get one small and one large resealable plastic bag. Pour the half-and-half, vanilla, and sugar into the small bag and seal tightly, pressing out excess air first. Fill the large bag halfway full of ice and add the salt. Put the small bag into the large bag, add some more ice, then seal the large bag tightly. Put on gloves and SHAKE THE BAG for 5 to 7 minutes. Remove the small bag, rinse with cold water, open carefully and enjoy the ice cream inside!

Chanukah

RAINBOW LATKES

When Chanukah rolls around, everyone's excited! There's candle-lighting, present-opening, dreidel-playing . . . and the food! To remember the miracle of the oil, we eat lots of foods fried in oil, like sweet sufganyot (donuts) and savory latkes (potato pancakes). Did you know you can make latkes out of other vegetables, too? Here's how to make a whole rainbow plate full of latkes!

For ORANGE latkes: 3 cups of shredded (peeled) sweet potato and 1 shredded carrot

For RED latkes: 3 medium beets, washed and peeled before shredding or finely dicing

How to Make
RAINBOW LATKES

DIRECTIONS and INGREDIENT NOTES:

For each batch of latkes, you'll need: 2 eggs; 1/2 cup flour or bread crumbs; 1/2 teaspoon salt; oil for frying. Optional: diced onions to taste; shredded potatoes to add that "classic" flavor (or make a golden batch!).

2 eggs

½ cup flour

½ teaspoon salt

Colorful veggies
(see notes)

Oil

Make each batch individually for a plateful of rainbow-colored latkes! For each different-colored latke batter, mix together the "for each batch" ingredients (except for the oil), then mix in the color ingredient. Form into patties, squeeze out any excess liquid, and then fry in the oil. This part is best for your grown-up to do: fry the latke patties for 2 to 4 minutes on each side until crisp and cooked through. Transfer latkes to a plate lined with paper towels to absorb excess oil, and let cool for a few minutes before serving.

For YELLOW latkes: ¼ cup yellow corn (canned or fresh) and 2 yellow squash (skin on, shredded)

For GREEN latkes: 2 medium green zucchinis (skin on, shredded)

For BLUE/INDIGO/VIOLET latkes: 1 large purple cauliflower

For E & M, because I love you and you are SO delicious
(but I promise not to REALLY eat you).

—Beth

To my pal, Brian

—Mike

SLEEPING BEAR PRESS™
2395 South Huron Parkway, Suite 200
Ann Arbor, MI 48104
www.sleepingbearpress.com

Printed and bound in China.

10 9 8 7 6 5 4 3 2 1

Library of Congress Cataloging-in-Publication Data

Names: Kander, Beth, author. | Moran, Mike (Illustrator), illustrator.
Title: Do not eat this book! : fun with Jewish foods & festivals /
written by Beth Kander ; illustrated by Mike Moran.
Description: Ann Arbor, MI : Sleeping Bear Press, [2023] |
Audience: Ages 4-8 years | Summary: "Rhyming text takes readers through
Jewish holidays, including Tu B'Shevat, Purim, and Chanukah, and their
related special dishes. Back matter includes a glossary describing each
holiday, along with easy, kid-friendly recipes of the featured dishes"
—Provided by publisher.
Identifiers: LCCN 2023000844 | ISBN 9781534111882 (hardcover)
Subjects: LCSH: Jewish cooking—Juvenile literature. | Fasts
and feasts—Judaism—Juvenile literature.
Classification: LCC TX724 .K359 2023 | DDC 641.5/676—dc23/eng/20230206
LC record available at https://lccn.loc.gov/2023000844